Carcassonne: The History and Legacy of th
in France's Fabled V

By Charles River Editors

Chen Siyuan's panorama of Carcassonne

About Charles River Editors

Charles River Editors is a boutique digital publishing company, specializing in bringing history back to life with educational and engaging books on a wide range of topics. Keep up to date with our new and free offerings with this 5 second sign up on our weekly mailing list, and visit Our Kindle Author Page to see other recently published Kindle titles.

We make these books for you and always want to know our readers' opinions, so we encourage you to leave reviews and look forward to publishing new and exciting titles each week.

Introduction

A medieval depiction of Cathars being expelled from Carcassonne in 1209

The Cathars

Carcassonne today is the capital of the Aude department in the Occitanie region of southwestern France, about 58 miles from Toulouse. It lies by the "eastward bend" of the glittering cobalt waters of the River Aude, which serves as a barrier between the two towns of the city: the Cité and the Ville Basse. It is the old Cité that attracts most of Carcassonne's visitors (3 million of them each year), for it houses the historic fortress that looks like it came straight out of a fairy tale and supposedly became the muse behind the captivating castles featured in Walt Disney's acclaimed 1959 classic *Sleeping Beauty*. But this breathtaking town is so much more than just the perfect spot for wedding shoots and social media narcissism, for it is a place that oozes medieval history.

Carcassonne: The History and Legacy of the Castles, Campaigns, and Crimes in France's Fabled Walled City examines the origins of the site and its sweeping history. Along with pictures depicting important people, places, and events, you will learn about Carcassonne like never before.

Carcassonne: The History and Legacy of the Castles, Campaigns, and Crimes in France's Fabled Walled City

About Charles River Editors

Introduction

    The Legend of Dame Carcas

    The Dawn of a Great Citadel

    The Treasures of Carcassonne

    Cathars and Crusaders

    Modern Developments

    Online Resources

    Bibliography

Free Books by Charles River Editors

Discounted Books by Charles River Editors

The Legend of Dame Carcas

"Yet could I these 2 days have spent,

While still the autumn sweetly shone,

Ah, me! I might have died content,

When I had looked on Carcassonne."

"Carcassonne," – French poet Gustave Nadaud, 1887

Posted by the Porte Narbonne, or Narbonne Gate, the entrance of the fabled La Cite in Carcassonne, is a striking bust that is often missed upon first glance, for it is overshadowed by the exquisitely preserved, millennia-old citadel in its background. But standing before the porte, her face draws one in – round, with plump cheeks, thin arches for eyebrows that follow the shape of her large, downturned eyes, wavy hair peeking out of her wimple – reminiscent of the "celestial" suns with human faces often seen in the bedroom décor of a hip, teenage girl from the '90s. Gaze upon her from a certain angle and distance, and it seems as if one of the iconic conical roofs behind her doubles as a russet-hued hennin.

Garbed in a fine gown with flower accents embroidered on her sleeves and a fussy wimple and veil, the joyfully radiant face that welcomes visitors into the citadel hardly appears to be the "heroine" type. Rather, the way she is depicted here is what usually springs to mind at the mention of a classic damsel in distress. That being said, while this particular damsel was indeed distressed, she relied on no one to not only save herself from the plight at hand, but the entire citadel itself.

This damsel, as inscribed on the plaque underneath the bust, is the beloved Dame Carcas, often billed by the locals as the star of the town's origin story.

A replica of Lady Carcas's bust

By the mid-8th century CE, the mighty Saracens from North Africa had conquered almost all of Spain, and having triumphantly trekked across the Pyrenees, they were well on their way to ticking off what is now the Occitanie region in southern France. The Moorish Emir Balaak, whose men seized the Carcassonnian castle shortly after their arrival, had moved into the spectacular complex, intending to make it his permanent residence.

Legend has it that the emir, though regarded by his enemies as a bloodthirsty, ruthless heathen of a prince, was anything but. Though aggressive and fearsome in times of war and conquest, Balaak, they say, was a compassionate, merciful man. Contrary to the rumors floating around the district, Balaak did not feast on the hearts of his prisoners, nor did he ornament the castle walls with the rotting, maggot-riddled corpses of his victims. He was charming, kind to his subjects, and reportedly even took it upon himself to educate the children of his prisoners in the "new science of mathematics."

His wife, the boundlessly wise and diversely gifted Dame Carcas, was just as, if not more adored by their subjects. Carcas was steadfastly loyal and attentive to the needs of her people and what she believed to be the greater good. Obey them, she vowed to her subjects, and no one in the kingdom will ever lay their head to rest with a bare stomach ever again.

The locals took her proposal to heart and heeded the word of their new rulers, and the royals fulfilled their end of the deal. Every echelon of society was well-fed, literacy was on the upswing, and despite the initially rough transition, peace reigned. That was, until Frankish King and Holy Roman Emperor Charlemagne began to experience a serious case of castle envy, and became increasingly resentful towards the warm reception Balaak and Carcas were apparently met with. Above all, the emperor refused to accept the idea of "infidel" sovereigns governing the magnificent Carcassonne, which he deemed to be God's land, and pledged to return her to her rightful owner.

Charlemagne, accompanied by a dozen of his trusty paladins and a tremendous battalion of close to 3,000 soldiers, charged down the Montagne Noire (Black Mountain) like a cascade of ants spilling out of their knoll, and headed for the citadel. Meanwhile, the guards from the watchtowers, who had spotted the alarming sight, alerted Balaak and Carcas, who in turn, ordered them to prepare their defenses at once. The Saracen soldiers scrambled into action, but within moments, they were surrounded.

A 9th century coin depicting Charlemagne

The citadel rumbled and rocked with the boulders and other projectiles slamming into the gates and walls of the threatened complex. Arrows and javelins rained from the sky, smiting the hapless soldiers and inhabitants stumbling over each other in the chaos. From the opposite side of the fortress walls came the riotous cries of the Roman soldiers, along with the echoing voice of their leader, Charlemagne, demanding for those inside to surrender.

Though clearly outnumbered, the Saracens, joined by the royals, clambered up to the ramparts and turrets and faced their foes head on. They hurled spears, reciprocated the arrows, and resorted to a series of creative defense tactics, such as hurling at them logs, rocks, and debris, and dumping barrels of boiling water, oil, molten lead, and feces over the walls. "The harder the harvest, the happier the reaper!" a red-faced Balaak reminded his men. "By Allah, my accomplices, we will greatly mow!"

As resolute in their defense as they were, the swiftly dwindling Saracens knew that they could not hold on for much longer. And so, a new plan was hatched. Taking with him what remained of the soldiers, Balaak bade the love of his life farewell and marched out of the citadel gates to confront the assailants, and hopefully, arrive at an understanding. Alas, it did not take long for the negotiations to go awry, and in the resulting bedlam, Balaak, along with every last one of his men, were slaughtered.

Carcas's heart shattered at the news of her husband's death. At the same time, she knew that her people now needed her more than ever, and could not afford for her to lose her head. She promptly gathered all the women, children, and the elderly, and decking them with whatever weapons were left strewn about, ordered them up to the ramparts.

Digging up and donning her husband's old gear, Carcas proceeded to strip the clothes and armor off the dead and dressed up dozens of straw mannequins, which she then placed in turrets and other strategic locations to give the appearance of a fully manned fortress. Utilizing all the knightly training she received as a young woman, she flitted from one mannequin to another, firing arrows and launching spears, scythes, odd rocks, and whatever else that was within reach. The resilient Saracen villagers' battle cries, coupled with Carcas' exceptional agility intimidated Charlemagne's troops into reluctance and inaction, who had (correctly) assumed that they had already killed the last of the Saracen warriors. Charlemagne was so astounded by his foes' hardiness that even he turned to his paladins and declared: "It is a miracle that the warriors continue to dwell there!"

Carcas's strategy, while ingenious, was not built for longevity; it would not take long before those inside began to run out of steam. Charlemagne's men had taken their water supply hostage, and obstructed all exits, thereby preventing any food and supplies from entering the citadel. Even so, as the story goes, Carcas succeeded in holding down the citadel for another 5 years.

Naturally, all things must come to an end. By the fifth year, all the wells inside were completely drained, and only about 30% of the population remained. Worse yet, the crops were long gone, and all the livestock – even pets – were slaughtered for sustenance, all but one bony pig and a tub of sweet corn. The villagers presented the last of the food to Carcas, but rather than sate her growling gut, she beckoned the pig forward, crammed it with sweet corn, and flung the squealing pig over the wall.

Carcas leaned over the parapet, and with bated breath, watched as the overstuffed pig burst on the ground upon impact, its stomach showering Charlemagne and other nearby knights with innards and undigested kernels of sweet corn. The dame delighted in the look of bafflement and defeat on the Christian soldiers' faces. Charlemagne seemed most distraught of all. He grumbled with rage, "This place is overflowing with food! How numerous and vigorous they must still be if they can still give wheat to the most vile beasts!" Believing that they had accomplished nothing with their siege, the dispirited Frankish troops turned around and began the long, grueling journey home.

Needless to say, Carcas was exhilarated by her unlikely victory, and in a fit of glee, she ran a lap around the city, ringing every bell from every tower. The silvery peals of the chiming bells were so loud that they drifted into the distance, and were heard by Charlemagne's men. One of the paladins galloped up to Charlemagne, frantically exclaiming, "Carcas sonne! (Carcas sounds!)" But the emperor, whose eardrums had practically been splintered by the deafening trebuchet blasts, failed to hear anything but the ringing in his ears, and he brushed it off as a collective hallucination. Others say Charlemagne heard the bells crystal-clear, but unable to fathom the thought of being outwitted by a woman, he feigned ignorance and simply told his men to march on, never again to look back...

This, the locals say, is how Carcassonne received her name, but as compelling as this tale is, it is exactly that. On top of the fact that the story fails to coincide with events established by ancient records and historians in the timeline of Carcassonnian history, Dame Carcas herself is a fictitious character, one of a rather modern invention. As maintained by Sylvie Caucanas, the Director of the Departmental Archives of Aude, Carcas made her first appearance in literature as an "allegorical figure" in a poem penned by Jean Dupré in 1534, wherein he creatively lists heroes and heroines that inspired the names of various countries and continents, such as Asia, Europe, Libya, and Mantua.

Be that as it may, this legend resides in a special place in the locals' hearts, for the heroine still lives on in many parts of Carcassonne today. Apart from the bust, there are streets, rustic inns and suites, as well as restaurants dedicated to her, such as the Auberge de Dame Carcas, or the "Hostel of the Dame Carcas." Attached to it is an eatery that serves an assortment of wines, dark coffees, cassoulet (a type of stew with pork skin and white beans), and honeyed pigs as a tribute to the swine that saved Carcassonne. In the local bakeries one will also find delicious almond cakes, or le petit carcassonnais," either shaped like castles, or clothed in castle-print wrappers, as well as tins of shortbread biscuits called the "friandises de Dame Carcas (Treats of Dame Carcas)."

The dame is also celebrated annually in the Château Comtal of the medieval citadel. In an effort to keep the tradition alive among the younger generations, the Center for French National Monuments hosts a weekend-long family-friendly extravaganza packed with various workshops, musical and dance performances, treasure hunts, and story-telling that revolved around the Dame's heroics. During Sunday teatime, a massive chocolate pig is carted out to the dining hall in the castle, where it is hammered apart to reveal, not sweet corn, but a horde of miniature chocolate piglets for the children to enjoy.

Of course, all of this still leaves questions. How was Carcassonne actually given its name, and what is it about this enchanting place that reels in millions of visitors every year?

The Dawn of a Great Citadel

"Petit a petit, l'oiseau fait son nid." ("Little by little, the bird makes its nest") – ancient French proverb

Even prehistoric humans seemed spellbound by the lush, tillable swathe of land that eventually became Carcassonne, for she appeared to be eternally blessed with pleasant weather, but it was her prime location that sealed the deal. If one were to stand atop her hill, one would be presented with a sweeping view of stunning mountain ranges, habitable valleys, and the verdant Aude plain, which would soon belong to her, and better yet, a bird's eye view of potential trade routes. What would one day become Carcassonne sat on a slab of land sandwiched between a route that connected the Atlantic Ocean to the Mediterranean Sea, and another that linked the Massif Central to the Pyrenees.

Little information exists about the Neolithic Iberians who archaeologists believe were indigenous to these parts. Prior to the break of the Neolithic Age, mankind roamed the earth with their families, both immediate and extended, as nomads. They were genuine free spirits, albeit more for necessity than for independence-seeking reasons, who lived in interim shelters and lived free of possessions, excluding a few weapons, tools, or whatever they could carry in a pouch. The men hunted beasts and the women collected edible plant life for the entire clan, which was to be consumed in the same day, lest the precious food be spoiled. Once resources dried up and food became scarce, or perhaps, to escape the unforgiving chills of the winter season, they wandered over to their next destination, never staying in one place for more than a couple of months.

The first Neolithic settlement in what is now Carcassonne is estimated to have sprung up sometime between 3500–3000 BCE. The rise of the new age brought about a revolutionary new way of life. These former nomads found permanent homes in this promising patch of land, and gradually developed a society to call their own. Capitalizing on the seemingly bottomless resources around them, they fashioned stone tools through the then-novel concepts of grinding and polishing. They experimented with and eventually created the art of farming, and rather than rely on hunting, learned to domesticate the beasts around them. The flourishing settlement also instituted a primitive version of weaving, as well as pottery making, the latter mostly used to store harvested crops.

About 2,300 years later, the land was inhabited by a tribe with Celtic-Gaulish roots known as the "Volques Tectosages." The tribe arrived first in the plain and valleys of Roussillon in the Eastern Pyrenees, and from there, poured westward to Toulouse, and later, to the area of Carcassonne. At this time, the land occupied by the Volques settlements, which sat on a plateau to the west of the modern-day Cité measured no more than 25 to 30 hectares (61.8 to 74 acres), just a sliver of the 6,509 hectares under Carcassonnian dominian today.

The tribesmen were among the first to punch deep pits into the earth, otherwise known as silos, to store their grain, which were later transformed into at least 500 silo towers. For shelter, they dwelled in small, simple huts constructed out of clay, straw, and stones, capped with tiled roofs. As innovative as they were, the Volques Tectosages were a superstitious people, and spent much of their time hoarding gold, silver, copper, amber, obsidian, lead ingots, gem stones, beads, and other currencies to appease their pagan gods; only by offering such valuables, they believed, would the gods smile down upon them and bless them with good weather and fortune.

Though much of their day was devoted to collecting these treasures for the gods, the Volques Tectosages opted to live plainly, with austerity and productivity at the core of their culture. Most worked in agriculture, collecting the grains stored in silos and crushing them with stones and wheels to produce cereals. Some tended growing herds of sheep, goats, and pigs. Others prowled about in the woods, hunting deer, boars, and other wild beasts.

Another portion of the population made their bread and butter in trade, working as merchants, clothes-spinners, craftsmen, and so forth. Ceramic workers and pot makers produced a wide array of everyday items, particularly vases, goblets, amphoras for wine and olive oil, and other containers. Blacksmiths produced weapons and tools out of bronze, copper, and iron, and supplied it to the traveling merchants, who then exported the items to Etruria, Greece, and the Iberian Peninsula. By the 7th century BCE, there was so much life in these lands that more than 9% of the previously undisturbed forested land was razed down to make room for more civilization.

A stretch of crudely made clay walls is presumed to have been installed around this vibrant and rapidly growing oppidum, which the locals named the "Carsac."

About a century later, Carsac was scrapped and abandoned. The inhabitants relocated to the nearby hilltop, and erected a new oppidum there. Having landed themselves one of the most coveted squares of land in all of the Languedoc region, the settlers wasted no time in assembling their defenses. First, another curtain of walls was established around the new town. For added security, a moat measuring about 6 meters (roughly 20 feet) wide and 2.5 meters (8.2 feet) deep bordered the walls surrounding the fortified town.

There was relative peace in the region for the next 400 years, punctuated by a few attempted invasions and minor territorial squabbles here and there, but tensions between the Romans and the inhabitants of central and southern France would soon trigger a major shift within the Carsac community. In the year 122 BCE, the Romans overpowered those in Provence and founded a colony by the Gulf of Lion. Once the colony was firmly established, the Romans journeyed south to Marseille, conquered the inhabitants there, and moved on to the Languedoc region, where they planted more Roman colonies.

It would not take long for the Romans to recognize the strategic significance of Carsac's coordinates. And so, in 100 BCE, the Roman vanquishers swam across the moat, scaled the bulwarks, and drove the inhabitants out of the hilltop. What remained of the natives were assimilated by Roman settlers – more specifically, the Colonia Narbo Martius – who went on to rename their new oppidum the "Colonia Julia Carcaso," or the "Colony of Julia Carcaso." It was later shortened to the more melodic "Carcasum."

By the last quarter of the 1st century BCE, the Roman Carcasum had blossomed into a full-fledged city, with the land on the foot of the hill now incorporated into its ever-growing territory. Carcasum was a thriving administrative and commercial center situated on the Aquitaine Way, and as the capital of the Julia Carcaso colony, presided over the western neck of the River Aude. Nestled between the towns of Narbo (Narbonne) and Tolosa (Toulouse), it was a bustling trading hub that saw the exchange of freshly picked wheat, barley, and other crops, cured meats, amphoras, metals, and sundries, some imported all the way from Montagne Noire, Corbières, and Rouergue.

To better guard their prosperous trading town from roaming pillagers, the Romans built the first stone walls that encircled Carcasum, which was essentially the debut of the Cité. These were the sturdiest bulwarks yet, zigzagging on for about 1,200 meters (1.2 kilometers) and reinforced with distinctive semi-circular towers and secured posterns. Archaeological remnants suggest that the site of Carcasum, at this stage, was no longer just a mere 74 acres but was estimated to have encompassed the bourns of the mountain, and it extended down to the northern end of what the locals called the "Narbonne-Toulouse Road."

While excavators have been unable to unearth any traces of the public buildings that existed during the Roman-Gallo period, hints of the original construction, including certain sections of the bulwarks, walls, and ramparts, are still visible in the modern fortress. As such, they were able to conclude that the bulwarks were pieced together with squared blocks of sandstone of roughly even weight, thickness, and height, rather than the usual tuff, a type of light, porous rock produced by condensed volcanic ash. The rubble surrounding the fragmented walls in the Roman ramparts on the northern end of the fortress reveal the thin, pale red pieces of the "fired clay" bricks used in their construction. The unique geometric mosaics that garnished the floors also indicate, though not concretely, that the buildings and houses built by the Romans were most likely orthogonal structures.

As it turns out, it was wise of the Romans to strengthen their defenses, for their greatest fear would one day be realized. The Romans at Carcasum managed to cling on to their fortress for a little over half a millennium until the Visigoths, spearheaded by King Theodoric II, conquered Gaul and declared Christianity the official religion, thereby transforming the site into a bishopric. It was in the year 453 CE (according to some sources, 436 CE) that the Visigoths ousted the Romans from Carcasum, which was soon renamed "Carcassonne." 9 years later, Septimania, the Roman predecessor of the Languedoc-Roussillon region, was ceded to the Visigoths.

Under Theodoric II, Carcassonne was converted to a frontier post, a border checkpoint of sorts for the northern neck of his kingdom. Apart from adding to the Roman-built fortifications and lengthening the crenellated bulwarks, the Visigothic king, a subscriber to Arian Christianity, built one of the first Christian churches in the area, dedicated to Alaric I, first king of the Visigoths. The church was later succeeded by a grand basilica constructed in honor of Saint Nazaire. Another namesake of his was a 2,000 foot tall emerald-green mountain not too far from the fringes of Carcassonne, the Montagne d'Alaric.

Vic Martin's picture of the mountain

A number of Visigothic leftovers help to shine a light upon their lifestyles. One of their cemeteries, for example, the Moural des Morts, which lies in the thick of a pine forest just 12 kilometers (7.5 miles) away from Carcassonne, is home to 44 stone tombs, laid out in "east to west" fashion. Judging by the size of these graves, even if one were to disregard those that belonged to children, the Visigoths were much smaller in stature compared to the size of an average adult today.

The vestiges of the Visigothic era also supported the fact that they were competent architects and builders, but they were lacking in terms of innovation. For the most part, they replicated Roman blueprints, and did little to improve upon them. That said, they worked expeditiously, and leeching off the designs of the subjugated, they assembled anywhere between 34-40 towers in their time. 2 of these towers, the chapel tower and the 92-ft Tower Pinte, loomed over all, the rest of the buildings in the area shivering in their shadows. In 485 CE, the newly crowned King Alaric II commissioned the renovation of the inner ramparts, instructing the builders to reinforce and expand upon the existing Roman structures.

It was only after securing the perimeters that the Visigoths began work on developing more settlements below the hilltop, which was known as the "Lower Empire," or today, the Ville Basse. The northern wing was absorbed into the fortifications by extending the bulwarks around them, and visitors can still make out the area of attachment by a castle gate known as "Le Bourg." It was here in this neighborhood that Christianity flourished, helping bring about a number of different Christian sects.

The Treasures of Carcassonne

"Who ought to be the king of France? The person who has the title, or the man who has the power?" – attributed to Pepin the Short

By the beginning of the 5th century CE, the western half of the Roman Empire was finding it almost impossible to stay afloat. In addition to an economic slump, the formerly flourishing empire found itself targeted by an onslaught of attacks from so-called barbarians, such as the Visigoths, the Ostrogoths, and the Huns. In 410 CE, the once indomitable city of Rome was held hostage by the Visigothic King Alaric. The standoff ended after a period of 3 days, but the humiliating event had tainted its reputation, and it took a noticeable toll on the Romans' morale. Western Roman authorities powered through for some time, but the abrupt deposition of Emperor Romulus Augustulus 66 years later by Flavius Odacer, who then rose to prominence as the first king of Italy, marked the disgraceful fall of the Western Roman Empire.

Following the dismantling of Western Roman Empire, the barbarian kings who had been eyeing the Roman lands competed to chisel out a chunk of the now defunct empire. Among these philistine monarchs was King Chlodovech, also known as King Clovis I. Not only would Clovis triumph in capturing Gaul, he fathered the famous Merovingian bloodline, otherwise known as the "long-haired kings," a driven dynasty that reigned for more than 200 years.

Clovis was no older than 15 when, upon the death of his father, King Childeric I, in 481, the crown of the Salian Franks was thrust unto him. Despite his young age, Clovis was determined to uphold his revered forerunner's legacy and do him proud.

The Salian Franks were first granted permission by the Romans to settle in the area of what is now Belgium around 358 CE, so long as they agreed to manufacture and equip the Roman soldiers and defend the border on their behalf. It was this relationship fostered by the Franks and the Romans that allowed for the piecemeal "Romanization" of the Franks. Like those who came before him, King Childeric aligned himself with the Romans, and captained numerous campaigns against the Visigoths, Saxons, and other barbaric Germanic tribes. His unswerving allegiance and loyalty to the Gallo-Romans earned their appreciation for him, so much so that several Roman officials inconvenienced themselves with travel to attend his elaborate funeral. Some even contributed to the hoard of weapons, jewels, gilded bees, 15 horses, and other fortunes buried alongside the royal casket.

By the time Clovis was brusquely seated upon the throne, the continent of Europe was a colorful patchwork of religious bodies. Arian Christians, Celtic Christians, Saracens, and pagan monarchs governed extensive strips of land, each committed to their own beliefs, and unreceptive to the then fledgling and wildly disorganized papacy. But the Roman papacy, though far from the powerhouse it would one day become, was every bit as ambitious as they were uncompromising about their creed.

Though the Ostrogoths, Visigoths, Vandals, Suebi, and Alans were technically Christians, they were disciples of Arius, a 4th century Christian presbyter based in Alexandria, Egypt. Arian Christians preached that Jesus, while possessing divine powers, was not divine himself, and was therefore "more than man, but less than God." As such, all Arians, Celtics, and other "new-age" Christian sects were promptly branded heretics by the Catholic Church. Their unorthodox views, and more importantly, their recalcitrance to the papacy was highly problematic for the Church, for this prevented them from bringing these irreverent and ungodly tribes, and in turn, their territories, under papal control.

Contrary to other Germanic tribes at the time, the Salian Franks were polytheistic pagans who bowed before a bevy of Germanic deities such as Wuotan (Odin), Zio (Mars), and Donar (Thor), among many others. Enter King Clovis I, and these longstanding traditions crumbled. Chroniclers say it was his consort, a Burgundian princess by the name of Clotilda, a devout Catholic in a family of Arians, who "showed him the light," so to speak. She badgered him endlessly about shedding his convictions and converting to the one true faith.

As told by historian Gregory of Tours, it was in the year 496 that a 30-year-old Clovis agreed to put his dear wife's faith to the test. If the Catholic deity were to ensure his victory over the Alemanni tribes in the Battle of Tolbiac in Germany, he would wash his hands of paganism for eternity and embrace Clotilda's god. Lo and behold, God seemingly did just that, because a few weeks later, the rival king was slain. Clovis's own army suffered crippling losses and barely emerged triumphant over his foes, but the Alemmani grudgingly raised their white flag not long after the loss of their king, and to Clovis, this was enough proof of God's existence. On the 25th of December that year, Clovis commemorated the birthday of Christ by submitting himself for baptism, which was performed by Bishop (and later Saint) Remigius in the cathedral of Reims.

A medieval depiction of the baptism

James Harvey Robinson, author of *An Introduction to the History of Western Europe*, succinctly summarizes the significance behind the baptism of the Frankish king: "With the conversion of Clovis, there was at least one barbarian leader with whom the Bishop of Rome could negotiate as with a faithful son of the Church...Certainly Clovis quickly learned to combine his own interests with those of the Church, and the alliance between the pope and the Frankish kings was destined to have a great influence upon the history of western Europe."

The religious discord between Clovis and the rising Arian superpowers, specifically the Visigoths, seeped into the 6th century. These non-secular battles are said to have been the first of its kind. As Henry Hart Milman, who authored *History of Latin Christianity*, put it, "For the first time, the diffusion of belief in the nature of the Godhead became the avowed pretext for the invasion of a neighboring territory."

Clovis, who now believed it was his purpose to bring these heretics to heel, initiated a string of military campaigns against these heathens, primarily pinning his focus on the Burgundians to the southeast of his kingdom. Ultimately, he was met with much resistance until 507, when he conquered the Visigoths at Vouillé in central France. Not only did his troops succeed in polishing off the Visigothic King Alaric II, the victory allowed him to annex a vast portion of southwest Gaul. Impressed by the crushing of the Visigoths, Eastern Roman Emperor Anastasius bestowed upon the Frankish king an honorary consulship, granting him authority over all other western kings.

Following the devastating defeat, which deprived them of their king, the surviving Visigoths scattered, taking refuge in the remaining Visigothic strongholds. His ego and confidence boosted by the victory at Vouillé, Clovis marched onward to Bordeaux, which he put down with little effort, and camped out there to escape the frigid cold of the winter. Once the ice had thawed, the Frankish troops proceeded to Aquitaine, and later, the Visigothic capital of Toulouse. They seized the territories there, swiping not only Visigothic domains but almost all of their treasure.

Carcassonne was, at this stage, considered a part of the Roman-conceived but now Visigoth-controlled Septimania, a district composed of the following bishoprics: Elne; Agne; Lodève; Béziers; Narbonne; Maguelonne; and Nimes; as well as the Aude and the Languedoc-Roussillon regions.

Some say it was simply Clovis' insatiable hunger for an even bigger kingdom that led him to direct his attention towards Carcassonne. It only made sense for Clovis to set his sights on Carcassonne, for it was no more than 60 miles from Toulouse, and it made for another convenient conquest. Then, there are those who claim that Carcassonne had been the Visigothic pearl the Frankish king had been after from the very beginning, since it supposedly sheltered the very treasure that King Alaric I had stolen from Rome during the sack of the Eternal City in 410.

The contents of the treasure remain a matter of dispute to this day. Some say it was a coffer sparkling with gold, silver, gems, and other stereotypical valuables of the like. The Church, on the other hand, insisted that the Visigoths had made off with the priceless "Treasure of Solomon," smuggled out of Jerusalem by the Romans themselves from the Temple of Solomon in the latter half of the 1st century CE. The scintillating spoils included a jewel-studded temple table for "showbread," 4 bronze bulls, a pair of cheribum sculptures, 2 magical gilded candlesticks with a sextet of grooved branches apiece (the Menorah), a medley of cups and vases made out of solid gold, priestly vestments, the Holy Veil, a missorium (a 500 pound diamond-encrusted dish made from pure gold), and other precious furniture.

In early 508, Clovis began the preparations for the attack on Carcassonne, but he did not know that God or good fortune would cease to smile upon him. Among his most grievous errors was charging his eldest son, Theuderic I, with pushing back the Visgothic forces in the Narbonensis and Rhone. While the 24-year-old showed plenty of promise when it came to partaking in battle, he was severely lacking in both the knowledge and experience needed to command it. Consequently, even with the assistance of Burgundian troops who joined him in Gondebaud, the Franks failed to secure the eastern provinces of the Visigoths.

Even so, Carcassonne was anything but unscathed. Frankish troops managed to surround the citadel, and though they were thwarted by the bulwarks, they succeeded in cutting off the Visigoths' water and food supplies for several weeks. In fact, the situation was at one point so dire that the panicking Visigoths reportedly tossed the treasure into the deepest well in the city, desperate to keep the irreplaceable relics out of Frankish hands. But just when it seemed as if the end was near, Theodoric the Great, King of the Ostrogoths and sole governor of Italy, came to the rescue, extending to them the last-minute aid that allowed the Visigoths to repel the Frankish forces.

Unwilling to jeopardize the blue-chip French territories he had worked so tirelessly to attain, Clovis chose to cut his losses and end the siege at Carcassonne. The Frankish troops retreated to Toulouse to regroup, and once their nerve was restored, they moved on to Angouleme, sinking their teeth into the last major town in Aquitaine. Only when Clovis was assured that the Visigoths would be powerless to stop him did he resume his conquests in the remaining areas of Southern Gaul left untrodden by the Franks. Clovis's men headed for Tours, brought the city under their yoke, and confiscated another cache of treasures.

Though Clovis ultimately decided to forgo conquering Septimania, he continued east and later north, declaring Paris his capital. He died in November 3 years later in what would become the City of Lights. By then, the capable king had conquered up to 75% of Gaul.

As per the conditions in the treaty agreed upon by Amalaric, the nephew and successor of the fallen Alaric II, and Athalric, grandson and successor of Theodoric the Great in the 520s, the Visigoths, though permitted to retain the last of their strongholds (including Carcassonne), were made to recognize the authority of the Italian king and present to him the treasures their ancestors had appropriated upon their conquests of the land. Rumor has it that the Visigoths coughed up only a fraction of the Carcassonnian treasure and continued to hold on to the most valuable of the loot, later transferring it to Spain when they finally departed Southern Gaul. But it appeared as if they, too, were not destined to be the last keepers of Solomon's treasure, for when the Saracens raided Spain, they stumbled upon some of the treasure, most notably the missorium and an ornate altar "made of a single emerald, surrounded by 3 rows of pearls, and supported by 60 feet of solid gold," said to be worth a whopping 500,000 gold pieces alone.

The Visigoths at Carcassonne began to fret when they received word that the capital of their Spanish strongholds, Toledo, had been overrun by invading Muslims in the early 8th century. In the years that followed, the Saracens continued their rampage up and down the length of the country, oftentimes assisted by bitter and forgotten natives who had their lands wrested from them by the vicious Visigoth intruders. By 714, they had established such a presence in the Iberian Peninsula that many began to refer to it by its Arabic moniker, "Al-Andalus." In just another 4 years, they would practically be in control of the entirety of the Northern Pyrenees. Their unexpected arrival and military dexterity took the Franks by surprise. The Franks, who had been forging forth with a similar campaign of their own at the time, had to delay their own ambitions for a time.

Barcelona and Narbonne – the latter situated on the Via Domitia, just 37 miles from Carcassonne – fell to the Saracen troops in the same year, 720, owing to the direction of Al-Samh ibn Malik al-Khawlani, the governor-general of the Al-Andalus. But this Saracen winning streak was interrupted the following year when they failed to capture Toulouse, and their plans were unraveled by the united Aquitanian and Frankish troops. The inglorious episode saw the slaughtering of up to 375,000 Muslim soldiers, Commander al-Khawlani included.

Though their defeat at Toulouse marked one of the worst military losses ever suffered by the Saracens, they remained undeterred. Returning to the Languedoc region in 725, they infiltrated and planted their flags in Carcassonne, Burgundy, and Autun.

For the next 34 years, Carcassonne, or as the Saracens christened it, "Karkashuna," or "Carcachouna," was occupied by the Muslim marauders. As for what exactly transpired in the year 759 is still up for speculation. Some revert to the legend of Dame Carcas, substituting Charlemagne with his father, Pepin the Short. While these myth-makers assert Pepin had singlehandedly driven the infidels out of Languedoc, he was outmaneuvered by the Saracen heroine and was thus unable to worm his way into the Carcassonnian fortress. The consensus among most historians, on the other hand, is that Pepin successfully lay siege to Carcassonne and "hounded the Arabs" out of the citadel.

The deaths of Pepin the Short and his younger brother, Carloman I, in 768 and 771 allowed Charlemagne to rule as the solitary king of the Franks. Among his first orders of business was to segregate the enormous empire he had inherited into the following districts: Aquitaine; Septimania (Carcassonne still included); and the Spanish March (later to become Barcelona). He then instituted a "comtal system" to better manage his empire, appointing officials, counts, viscounts, and bishops as the governors of these lands. In exchange for the authority and slew of privileges awarded to them, the counts and viscounts pledged to surrender a majority of the taxes collected to the Frankish crown, and they were permanently on call to defend their lands and other Frankish territories if needed. The first Count of Carcassonne was a noble only known as Bello, the patriarch of the Bellonids, a distinguished dynasty that filled prestigious comtal posts in Catalonia and Septimania for centuries.

Naturally, mastery over the honores (gifts of office, i.e., bishops, counts, and so forth) progressively weakened after Charlemagne's death in late January 814. Frankish territories in the outskirts of the empire leapt on the opportunity to detach themselves from the shriveling empire, eventually securing their independence. Observing this turn of events, the honores, too, began to itch for their independence. The affluent noble dynasties now regarded the lands entrusted to them as "hereditary possessions," leading to the rise of a "territorial aristocracy."

The third-in-line to the Carolingian lineage that ruled Carcassonne and Razès was the grandson of Bello, Oliba II. He envisioned the merging of these territories into the County of Barcelona, but it was only following his demise that the system of inheriting honores titles was officially installed. Upon the death of Count Acfred II in 934, the spawn of Oliba II, Carcassonne was passed onto his daughter, Arsenda. The heiress' marriage to Arnold, the Count of Comminges, automatically rendered Carcassonne a realm of Comminges County.

In the decades that followed, the Counts of Comminges preserved the tradition of nepotism that ran rampant across the Midi, unabashedly packing their councils and governments with their sons, brothers, cousins, nephews, and relatives. Finally, in 1068, Count Peter Raymond II broke tradition by divvying up Carcassonne between his 3 daughters.

A year later, all 3 daughters advertised their rights to the twin counties of Carcassonne and Razès, and Agde and Béziers, on the Midi market. Counts from near and far immediately pounced and jostled for the bait, but eventually it was awarded to Count Raymond Berengar I of Barcelona, who presented the enterprising sisters with the most appealing offer: an astounding total of 4,000 mancusos (400 ounces of solid gold). Not long after the deal was sealed, Viscount Raymond Bernard of Albi and Nimes, who was betrothed to Ermengarde, one of the 3 viscountesses, was named the Viscount of Carcassonne. He ruled as such until his brother, Bernard Aton Trencavel, then the Viscount of Albi, Nimes, and Béziers, assumed the distinction in 1082.

Between the years of 1082 and 1209, Carcassonne experienced pivotal progress and expansion under the guardianship of the Trencavels. Besides the further development of city infrastructure and the constellation of construction projects that were commissioned and completed under their watch, the local industries, which centered on wool and wine-making, burgeoned. The robust and continuously growing economy allowed authorities to increase tolls and taxes – at times amounting to half the value of the commodity – which in turn, fattened up the Carcassonnian treasury.

In the 1120s, Bernard Aton, otherwise known as Bernard Ato IV, ordered the construction of the Viscount's castle, or as the locals called it, the "Chateau Comtal." The site of the grandiose project, which dragged on until 1229, was outlined on a square of land on the western end of the hilltop, "on the highest point of the city." The castle itself comprised 2 spacious, single-story buildings, a lofty square tower, "arranged at right angles," hemmed in by wooden palisades on the eastern wing of the castle. Due to the length of its construction, the Chateau Comtal is flavored with a variety of architectural styles, ranging from medieval aesthetics to Romanesque and Gothic touches. The Chapel Sainte-Marie, constructed in 1150, was the private prayer house of the viscounts, and some of the chapel's original semi-circular apse remains visible to this day.

The chateau was shielded by a circuit of crenellated defensive walls, armed with its own set of round watchtowers that guarded the main and rear entrances. The spaces between the rectangular crenellations were used as mountings for archers and other soldiers armed with boulders, boiling oil, and other defenses, with the parapets themselves serving as an efficient screen against the enemies from below. The sturdy stone drawbridge that served as a plank over the cavernous dry moat was raised during times of incursion and war, sealing the castle shut.

On June 12, 1096, Pope Urban II popped into Carcassonne to consecrate the cornerstone and building materials of a new cathedral there, later unveiled as the "Basilique Saint Nazaire and Saint Celse." The new basilica, which was built atop the foundations of the Frankish church there, would one day become a local landmark, fondly nicknamed the "Jewel of Carcassonne" by the locals.

A statue of Pope Urban Ii in France

In the 1240s, the cathedral underwent a drastic makeover, and was rebuilt in the Gothic style, as ordered by the episcopates of Pierre Rodier and Pierre de Rochefort, and authorized by French King Philip III. The crypt tucked away in the basement of the basilica was added in the late 13th century. It went on to serve as the official church of Carcassonne until the 1800s.

The majestic sandstone structure amazed those who laid their eyes upon it. Its yellow brick facade, crowned with miniature crosses, and adorned with floral cutouts, seemed to shimmer under the sunlight, as if coated with a layer of gold. The layout of the cathedral itself was shaped like a Latin cross, measuring about 59 meters (194 feet) from one end to the other. The transepts, or arms of the church, were about 36 meters (118 feet) in length, and the nave, which housed the congregation, about 16 meters (52.5 feet) in width. Last, but not least, was arguably the highlight of the cathedral – its gorgeous collection of delicate stained glass windows. Apart from the ornamental windows that cast dreamy, rainbow-like shadows in floral and geometric patterns on the floors of the church, were the floor-length windows featuring 16 biblical scenes pertaining to Christ, such as the Adoration of the Magi, the Crucifixion, and the Descent of the Cross, among others. The whimsical gargoyle water spouts sprinkled about the church are yet another feature that grips the attention of all visitors alike.

Dreading another repeat of history, the Trencavels erected the last line of defense in the early 12th century, around the year 1130. The moat was deepened, and the winding bulwark that fenced in the Cité was augmented so that it was now more than twice the length of the Roman wall, expanding from 1,200 meters to over 3,000 (1.86 miles). Another 13-19 towers, topped with terracotta-tiled roofs were added to the new segments of the bulwarks, so that it now amounted to a total of 53. The 4 barbicans mounted onto the 4 gates of the city were patched up and reinforced. Matacanes, or hoardings, which were either ring-shaped wooden galleries or tunnel-like passageways hovering 130 feet above ground, were also built. These allowed for soldiers to launch missiles and other projectiles at their assailants below.

A picture of the fortified wall

A picture of a reconstructed hoarding at Carcassonne

The Cité was also split into 16 châtellenies, or lordships. Each châtelain was to guard 1 or 2 towers, as well as the parts of the bulwark that flanked the towers in question. A pair of boroughs, Saint Michael and Saint Vincent, each a component of the 16 châtellenies, were established just outside the Carcassonnian borders. Inhabitants and soldiers stationed there were also expected to maintain the castles and defenses assigned to them for extra security.

Cathars and Crusaders

"L'habit ne fait pas le moine." ("The vestment does not make the monk") – an ancient French proverb

"The Roman Church...[says] that the heretics they persecute are the church of wolves. But this is absurd, for the wolves have always pursued and killed the sheep, and today it would have to be the other way around for the sheep to be so mad as to bite, pursue, and kill the wolves, and for the wolves to be so patient as to let the sheep devour them!" – from the alleged writings of the Cathars

Medieval France was a disorderly hodgepodge of kingdoms, dukedoms, fiefs, and counties. The confusion in governance was only amplified by the crisscrossing alliances and religious beliefs held by the local leaders there. The instability in southern France was especially exacerbated by the ill-defined limits of authority, not to mention the convoluted relations between the rulers.

Parts of Languedoc were labeled as fiefs of the Holy Roman Empire and regulated by the Catholic Church. There were some that paid tribute to Aragonese sovereigns, and others that answered only to the French Crown. Then, there were who that held firm to their independence, batting away all attempts of intervention from foreign monarchs. The Count of Toulouse, a vassal of the Aragonese Crown, owned the most fruitful and substantial tracts of land in Languedoc, and as such, he was hailed as the most powerful man in all of Southern France.

It was the democratic governing styles of the Counts of Toulouse, Carcassonne, and other like-minded leaders that made them popular among their subjects. They were champions of religious tolerance who received immigrants and refugees with open arms. The diversity of their communities – which only grew more diverse by "exotic" foreigners in search of a safe space for worship – worked wonders for the local economies and paved the way to advancements in literature, technology, medicine, and general societal growth. The golden age simultaneously experienced by the Languedocian counties at this time might have reached even further heights had it not been for the meddling Catholic Church.

The skyrocketing complaints about the Roman clergy's fear-mongering, lawlessness, dereliction of duties, and vindictiveness in Languedoc were instrumental in the breeding of the dissenters in the region, but no other cult would strike a louder chord with the disgruntled locals than the Cathars. The Cathars, a dualist Gnostic sect, vowed to bring about the comeback of the "Early Church." The Catholics vehemently condemned these heretics for their unconventional beliefs, which chiefly preoccupied with the concept of 2 gods: a benevolent God of love, kindness, salvation, and all that is good, and a malevolent god, who reigned over the material world. Numerous historians and other non-Catholics, however, are adamant that it was the Cathars' vocal opposition about the flagrant corruption and dishonest practices of the Church, such as their collection of tithes, peddling of "sacred" burial spots and indulgences, that made the Cathars the brightest and most erratically blinking blip on the Church's radar.

As the reputation of the Catholic Church in the Languedoc continued to decay, the Cathars seized the opportunity to further their expansion in the area. Toulouse was among the first names on the Cathar agenda. The goodwill and acceptance exhibited by the liberal leaders allowed the Cathar population there to grow, swelling to close to twice its starting size in just a matter of months.

Count Raymond VI of Toulouse was a certified Catholic, which made his sympathy towards the Cathars and other heretics all the more incongruous with the norm. Though incongruous, it was not surprising, for most of his relatives, as well as key members in his entourage, identified as Cathars. As keenly lauded as he was by the citizens of Toulouse, the Catholic Church was more than frustrated by Raymond's insistence on fraternizing with the enemies. They grew even more appalled upon learning that the count's cabinet and councils were made up almost equally of Catholics, Cathars, and Jews.

Raymond VI's seal

In an ideal world, Count Raymond would have most likely ignored the grating criticisms of the Church, but his complicated and unbreakable ties to the neighboring kingdoms prevented him from doing so. Though the majority of the lands in Toulouse were domains of the Aragonese kingdom, the count also held territories in Provence and other areas in southeastern France, granted to him by the French and English monarchs, and most significantly, the Holy Roman Emperor. Raymond strove to maintain the order within his bickering territories, but the disoriented and increasingly belligerent Church would soon back him into a corner.

From Toulouse, the Cathars' beliefs spread about 50 miles northeast to the city of Albi. Here, the Cathars developed such a daunting presence that the Catholics erroneously concluded it to be the center of the heretical faith. In fact, the same misconception led to the term "Cathars" being used interchangeably with "Albigensians."

Once a stable stronghold was established in Albi in the early 12th century, Catharism spread about 67 miles south to Carcassonne. Like those in Toulouse and Albi, the infuriated Carcassonnians were intensely dissatisfied with the performance of the Catholic Church, and many did not think twice about jumping the sinking ship.

It was in 1207 that the tensions between the Cathars and the Catholics inevitably came to a head, and Carcassonne would find itself inescapably enmeshed in the chaos. The nobility in Languedoc waged war against one another over territorial disputes, with many of their campaigns partly financed by the Count Raymond, but as these home-grown battles devolved further into disarray, the aggravated mercenary employers began to take issue with their liege lord. Relations between the parties were so strained that the commanders deliberately refrained from informing Count Raymond of Peter of Castelnau's visit that year. The delegate had been dispatched by the papacy to conduct a chain of meetings with the Catholic nobles in the hopes of coaxing them into discontinuing their territorial wars. Instead, he urged them to work jointly towards squashing the Cathars instead.

It did not take much to persuade the commanders of these domestic battles to suspend their infighting, but luring Raymond was another matter. As to be expected, the count refused to cooperate, and he was livid about the inconstancy of his liege subjects. Not only did their insubordinate decision put his plans for expansion on pause, he could not stomach the thought of his people being subjected to such discrimination and harassment.

It soon dawned on Raymond that he was the odd man out. Even so, he fought to reverse the plans of the Catholic Church, but to no avail. Raymond was subjected to a resounding declaration of excommunication, the mortifying experience of a public whipping (which left him exposed to the cruelties of mob justice), and the withdrawal of support from his trusted officials and other Languedocian nobility. Unable to withstand the pressure, the Count issued a groveling apology to the Church in early August of 1207, and to their delight, he pledged to exterminate every last one of the Cathars in Languedoc.

As it turned out, Raymond's words were far louder than his actions. He warded off papal representatives sent to collect reports on the annihilation of the Languedocian Cathars, each excuse more halfhearted than the last. When the papacy decided that they would no longer stand for Raymond's intentional inertia on the matter, the irate Church severed all ties with him once again and imposed upon him a barrage of charges, his most unforgivable crime being his condoning of the Cathars.

By January 1208, Raymond, now at his wit's end, summoned Peter of Castelnau to his estate in Saint Gilles. He plied Peter with plenty of food and drink and lavished him with hospitality in an effort to convince the delegate to act as a mediator with his superiors on his behalf. In the days that followed, Peter listened patiently as Raymond aired his grievances, but under strict instructions himself, he remained immovable at the negotiating table. Embittered by the static progress of their roundabout discussions, both parties became growingly combative. Their last meeting, which took place on the 15th of that month, was so contentious that Raymond lost his cool and took a swing at him.

Shaken, Peter left the count's estate, with Raymond still cursing up a storm behind him, and his day would only take a turn for the worse. Still seething over his altercation with the count, Peter failed to detect the ominous figure creeping up behind him. When he finally did spot the sinister shadow tailing him, it was too late for him to stop the assailant from plunging a dagger into his back. The assailant scurried off as quickly as he came, leaving a gurgling Peter to bleed out on the corner of the street opposite of Saint Gilles Abbey.

Though the assailant was never identified, Pope Innocent III was the first to point a finger in Raymond's direction. Luckily for Raymond, due to the lackluster weight of his hearsay-based evidence and unsubstantiated claims, not to mention the absence of witnesses, he was never brought to trial.

Pope Innocent III

That said, the murder of Peter of Castelnau was enough to provoke the already restless pope into waging a full-scale war against the Cathars. On March 10, 1208, the day of Peter's canonization, the pope summoned the Christian Crusaders and unleashed upon them a riveting, albeit long-winded, speech: "Forward then, Christian knights! Forward, courageous recruits of the Christian army! May a pious zeal set you on fire to avenge so great an offense against your God!...The ship of the Church will suffer total shipwreck unless it gets some strong help in this unprecedented storm. This is why...we order you...in the name of Christ, in the face of such peril, we promise the remission of your sins, so that you may thwart such dangers without delay."

The pope urged them to unshackle all inhibitions and shed all restraints when dealing with these heathens: "Be diligent to destroy the heresy by any means God will inspire you to use. With greater assurance than with the Saracens, since they are more dangerous, fight the heretics with a mighty hand, and an outstretched arm...Strip them of their land, so that Catholics may replace the eliminated heretics and serve in God's presence...according to the discipline of your orthodox faith."

Even the pope himself would later admit that there existed no evidence tying Raymond, or any other Cathar, to the cold-blooded murder. Others accused the Catholic Church of choreographing and executing the assassination themselves in a desperate bid to justify violence against the heretics, but they, too, had no concrete evidence.

Whatever the case, the Catholics proceeded with their campaign, and in 1209, the Albigensian Crusade began.

The first Catholic battalion of about 10,000–20,000 strong began their march south from Lyon in early spring of that year. Leading the crusade was Simon de Montfort, an English-French aristocrat and seasoned military general. Assisting him in this momentous campaign were the Counts of Saint-Pol and Nevers, the Seneschal of Anjou, the Duke of Burgundy, and other veteran captains with equally glittering careers.

The party continued to slog through the rough terrain along the River Rhone, heading for Provence, where they were later united with the "Spiritual Adviser" of the Crusade, Arnaud Amalric. This was the same Arnaud Amalric who, when asked how to distinguish between the Cathars and Catholics, reportedly uttered the famous phrase now most commonly associated with the Albigensian Crusade: "Kill them all. The Lord will recognize His own."

The Catholic forces laid siege to Cathar Country with ease, and in late July the Cathars experienced the magnitude of the crusaders' savagery for the first time. On the 21st of that month, Catholic troops descended upon the Langudeocian town of Béziers, which was under the guardianship of Raymond-Roger Trencavel III, the Viscount of Béziers and Carcassonne. Trencavel stepped forward to receive the Catholic generals at once, and when he failed to reach an understanding with them, alerted his uncle, the Count of Toulouse, and petitioned him for help. To Trencavel's consternation, not only did Raymond decline, many of the Count's own soldiers had been integrated into the same Catholic troops stationed at Béziers.

The Catholic generals demanded from Trencavel a list of 222 Cathars – evidently, to fill a quota they had been provided by the Church – but to this, Trencavel refused. The next morning, tens of thousands of Catholic soldiers surrounded the Basilica of St. Mary Magdalene, where 20,000 locals gathered for Mass, bolted it shut, and promptly torched the place. All men, women, and children perished in the flames. When the soldiers later learned that they would not be keeping the plunder from Béziers - it would instead be used to fund the ongoing crusade - the seething soldiers rioted and razed the city to the ground.

A medieval depiction of the pope excommunicating the Cathars and the Catholics massacring them

Béziers was still steeped in smoke and fresh rubble when the crusaders marched onto their next target: Carcassonne. The papal-endorsed soldiers broke past the Carcassonnian borders on the 1st of August and positioned themselves on various ends of the bulwark, priming their trebuchets. On the opposite side of the walls, Carcassonnian warriors hastened to their assigned towers, some loading their own catapults with boulders, and others, strapped with bows and arrows, shimmying up to the ramparts. They did their best to ride the high of the adrenaline, but the stifling air was fraught with fear, for they had heard about the massacre in their sister town.

Though Raymond-Roger had witnessed the savagery of the crusaders at Béziers firsthand, he refused to capitulate to the Church's demands. The Carcassonnians put up a fierce fight, fending off the invaders with numerous sorties and flicking off the soldiers attempting to scale the bulwarks time and time again. But they could not repel them forever.

As with every siege, the crusaders girdled the River Aude, cutting off the county's access to clean water. The Carcassonnians, who were now well-versed in siege warfare, were no strangers to this tactic. They initially stood their ground, relying on their limited supply of wells and ignoring their grumbling guts. By the next week, however, their spirits had been reduced almost completely, and their morale was close to disintegrating.

Fortunately for the Carcassonnians, trashing the town and razing it to the ground was not an option for the treasure-hunting Catholics, having learned their lesson from Béziers. The Catholic commanders called upon Raymond-Roger once more and presented to him a new ultimatum - the Carcassonians could either prolong this unwinnable war, or they vacate the premises voluntarily and unharmed, leaving behind all their possessions.

The viscount grappled with the equally unfavorable choices he was given, but unwilling to risk the lives of any more of his diminishing subjects, he threw in the towel on the 15th of August. In the weeks that followed, crestfallen Carcassonnians filed out of the citadel, carrying "nothing but their sins" on their backs. Raymond-Roger was scheduled to follow suit, but he was struck with a change of heart, the reality of his debilitating losses sinking in at the last second. The viscount resisted, and as a result, he was immediately shackled and carted off to the dungeon of his own fortress. Catholic historians say it was a mix of the trauma, as well as complications from dysentery, that killed him weeks later at the tender age of 24. Skeptics, on the other hand, going by the rumors that circulated during this time, contend that he was murdered by his captors.

Following the untimely death of Viscount Raymond-Roger, Simon de Montfort was appointed to replace him. He tasked builders and laborers with repairing the damaged sites of the city and identifying the flaws in the Carcassonnian defenses, many of which were exploited by the crusaders during the siege. With that, he drew up plans to set them right.

Now that the viscountcy lay in the hands of the Catholic Church, the papacy took advantage of the existing facilities and converted what was once a Cathar sanctuary into a veritable house of horrors designed to torture those it had once protected. At least 2 of the Carcassonnian towers were recast as "Inquisition Towers" for the Catholic Church.

The Inquisition, which was conceived in Languedoc by Pope Lucius III in 1184, was rebooted in 1233 by Pope Gregorious IX. Inquisitors – mostly Dominicans – were vested with the power to conduct "inquiries" into the lives of accused heretics. Worse yet, the merciless Inquisitors were given free rein to dole out whatever punishments they saw fit, and all the better if the punishments were crueler.

The tower next to the Porte Aude was the first to be transformed into a torture chamber. Its ground floor was connected to the overhanging passageway leading to the Tower of Justice, now known as the "Gallery of the Inquisition," which contained a comprehensive library of files and records dutifully kept by the operators of the dungeon. A scathing letter addressed to Jean Galand in 1285, a Dominican Inquisitor based in Carcassonne, elaborates on the atrocities experienced by those imprisoned there. "You have created a prison called 'the Wall,' which would be better called 'Hell,'" wrote the Consuls of Carcassonne. "In it you have constructed small cells to inflict pain and to mistreat people using various types of torture. Some prisoners remain in fetters...and are unable to move. They excrete and urinate where they are... Some are placed on the chevelt; many of them have lost the use of their limbs because of the severity of the torture... Life for them is an agony, and death a relief. Under these constraints they affirm as true what is false, preferring to die once than to be thus tortured multiple times..."

The Crusaders went on to enjoy an uninterrupted winning streak for the next six years, and though the Cathars managed to muster up the strength and manpower to defend themselves effectively, even reclaiming most of the lands they had been robbed of by 1225, their "victories" were short-lived. Just four years later, Languedoc was absorbed into the French kingdom, and a new type of operation to eliminate the heretics was unveiled in the form of the Inquisition.

Considering the skyrocketing number of bizarre and disturbing rumors that hounded the heretics in the 13th century, it seemed as if the Catholics had created a department solely dedicated to churning out anti-Cathar propaganda. First and foremost, they capitalized on the death of Peter of Castelnau and the gullibility of the grieving followers. When commemorating Peter's death, whom they now hailed as a "martyr," they concluded their poignant accolades with his last words: "May God forgive thee, brother, as I fully forgive thee." It did not matter that there were no witnesses to his death – the Catholics accepted this as fact.

Apart from vilifying the Cathars as callous and heartless murderers, the Catholics used what little they knew about Cathar doctrine, twisting truths to further their agenda. Due to the Cathars' unorthodox views on sex and marriage, they were accused of being chronic masturbators, and engaging in incest, bestiality, and other unthinkable acts. They were branded as sodomites, often using the Cathars' preference to travel in duos of the same gender as proof. The Catholics themselves, including many a pope, were also no strangers to the "crime" of sodomy, but to them, of course, that was neither here nor there.

The year 1231 marked the beginning of the Inquisition against the Cathars in southern France. Three religious judges (titled "commissioners") were to be sent to each parish, and Catharism was to be uprooted. There, they would, as dictated by the Council of Toulouse in 1229, be "specially charged with seeking out the heretics from the cellar to the attic, and denouncing them to the bailiffs."

Bailiffs and interrogates sent by the Inquisitors were then tasked with conducting "interviews" with suspected Cathars. Those deemed guilty were afforded a "grace period" of two days to publicly denounce their heretical faiths and convert to the one "true" version of Christianity. Those who capitulated were met with mercy and released with a warning. That said, these first-time offenders were made to don, "from now on and forever," a pair of bright yellow cross measuring about 10 inches on their chests and collars, as a permanent reminder of the deplorable sin they had committed. As degrading as these distinctive badges of shame – or as the locals called them, "las debanadoras," or "winders" – were, the Cathars made sure to have them pinned onto them at all times, for failure to do so could earn one a second conviction, which meant the death penalty.

Cathars who refused to renounce their faiths were taken to trial, where they were to be tried by two chief Inquisitors, the Lord of the land, and other local court officials. Inquisitors presented to the court the evidence against the accused, which typically came in the form of testimonies, spy reports, and so on, until the Cathar made a full confession. It was then that the Cathar was passed off to state authorities, who settled upon an "appropriate" punishment for the heretic.

Some of the convicted were imprisoned, as instructed by the Catholic Church: "Every heretic whose conversion was not obtained by devotion but by fear of the laws, be detained in a fortress, so that he cannot defile others…" Though sentenced to life in prison, the conditions in these dungeons were so abysmal that many quickly met with death. Conversely, Cathars deemed "unsalvageable," as well as second-time offenders, were fed to the flames. Some were thrust into burning buildings, asphyxiating before the flames devoured their corpses. Others were tethered to stakes and engulfed by the raging bonfire. These methods of execution by fire only became more creative with time. Such methods included the frying of Cathars in drums of sulfur, resin, and oil. On other occasions, the Catholics roasted the heretics alive in ovens or broiled them on gridirons.

A depiction of Cathars being burned at the stake

The Inquisitors' obsession with the Cathars was so frightening that both Cathars and non-Cathars lived in equal fear for their lives. Many were convicted solely on the testimonies of their neighbors, who were often incentivized by their own safety. The lax requirements for these testimonies also gave way to numerous grudge-bearers exacting their revenge on business rivals and enemies. After all, even if their testimonies were disproven, they could be let off the hook by simply stating that they had been innocently misguided by their "zeal for the Faith."

Upon the death of the Cathar, half – and in many cases, all – of his or her property, which was previously to be passed on to their surviving family members, was confiscated by the Church. Soon, the Church, as suggested by the Dominicans, began to administer postmortem trials. Those found guilty of Catharism were dug up and stripped of their valuables, and their assets were taken from their heirs.

Raymond II de Trencavel, the son of Viscount Raymond-Roger, was only 2 years old when his father wasted away behind bars. That being said, given all the tales (both tall and true) surrounding Raymond-Roger's heroics, which were naturally shared in droves following his demise, it was as if the son had known the father all his life. As a matter of fact, many say it was these very tales that inspired the junior Raymond to take back what he believed rightfully belonged to his father.

In hindsight, many believe it was Raymond's restlessness that contributed to the downfall of his overzealous ambitions. The Viscount of Béziers made his affinity with the surviving Cathars, Jews, and other "heretics" in the county no secret, which quickly made him a recipient of unwanted attention from the Catholic Church. The hawk-eyed Inquisitors were watching him long before he even concocted his daring scheme.

On September 17, 1240, a band of soldiers from Béziers galloped towards Carcassonne and formed a blockade around the fortress. For weeks, Raymond's men warred with the besieged occupants of Carcassonne. And while they came close to knocking down a stretch of the fortress walls, the Catholics at Carcassonne, who had been expecting them, were swiftly rescued by relief forces of the royal army.

Raymond's troops managed to keep the unanticipated reinforcement at bay for some time, but they were eventually chased away to Montreal. The relentless royal forces followed them there, and tormented him with yet another siege. Unlike his father, Raymond managed to evade his enemies by the skin of his teeth, and took refuge in Barcelona. Still, Raymond's territories never truly recovered. Not only would he fail to retrieve Carcassonne in the name of his father, he was left with no choice but to surrender Béziers and the rest of his lands to King Louis IX in 1247.

As decreed by the French king, all inhabitants were cleared out of the Cité and prohibited from returning for 7 years. Louis then marshaled a team of veteran soldiers and architects, and charged them with repairing and boosting the defenses of the fortress. A substantial garrison was also installed to defend the citadel from rebellious Catalan or Aragonese soldiers, Cathar sympathizers, and other allies of Raymond looking to seize the fortress for the disgraced viscount.

The quintet of "Cathar Castles" that stood by the boundary between the Trencavel and Aragonese-owned Roussillon possessions were among the properties Viscount Raymond II was made to relinquish. Each castle was overhauled and redeveloped as "frontier fortresses," or "royal citadels," kitted out with a royal garrison of their own. They were then reintroduced as the "cinq fils de Carcassonne," or in English, the "Five Sons of Carcassonne": the Château de Peyrepertuse, Château de Puilaurens, Château d'Aguilar, Château de Termes, and the Château de Quéribus.

In 1248, the displaced Carcassonnians that been banished from the Cité began work on a new community across the River Aude. This was none other than the Ville Basse, or "Lower Town," also known as the "Bastide of Saint Louis." The Ville Basse, which came with a network of parallel streets and an unusual graveyard above one of the bastions on the bulwark, would one day become the commercial center of Carcassonne. By the mid-1300s, there were an estimated 7,000 or so houses in the booming industrial district – complete with its own consulate – of the Ville Basse alone. Meanwhile, the "Old City" remained free of civilians, and now served as the "episcopal see and inquisitorial seat" of Carcassonne.

In 1315, the French crown ordered the construction of "Le Pont Vieux" (The Old Bridge). The new structure, which was funded by a special tax and completed 5 years later, was built atop the foundations of the Roman bridge. Simply designed, the drab gray bridge consisted of a straight walkway, shored up by a dozen brick arches measuring about 10 to 14 meters (33 to 46 feet) across each. Apart from linking and delineating the border between the Cité and the Ville Basse, the neutral status of the Pont Vieux made it the setting for many peace treaties and truces signed by the feuding residents of the Carcassonnian districts.

While the death toll that resulted from the Inquisition in Carcassonne paled greatly in comparison to the neighboring counties and viscountcies, it was, to the locals, a cancerous presence they strove to eliminate. In 1303, just 12 years before the construction of the Point Vieux, the Carcassonnians finally achieved what they were beginning to think was an unattainable feat.

It was Bernard Délicieux, the prior of a Franciscan convent in the viscountcy, who many credit with driving the Inquisitors out of Carcassonne. Troubled by the unchecked powers of the Inquisitors and the unnecessarily cruel torture the persecuted were made to endure, Bernard criticized the Church in ecclesiastical meetings, and pleaded with them to change their ways. When his protests continued to go unheard, Bernard organized a revolt against the institution in 1299, which triumphed in preventing the Catholic guards from getting to the 2 heretics he had stowed away in his convent. He went on to raise another ruckus in July of the following year when the Inquisitors exhumed Castel Fabre, a member of the wealthy bourgeois, and attempted to brand him a Cathar in a bid to seize his possessions from the deceased's descendants.

In October 1301, Bernard, partnering with Jean de Picquigny, the new viceroy of Languedoc, journeyed to the royal residence of King Philip IV. There, they presented to the king a document brimming with proof of the corruptions of the Inquisitors, more specifically, those of Bishop Castanet and Friar Foulques de Saint-Georges. Not "even babies in their cradles," were safe, insisted an unnamed witness, were safe from the Inquisitors.

Bernard and Jean were initially ignored by the French king, who belonged to the same camp as the Inquisitors, but when the complaints involving the 2 head inquisitors continued to mount, King Philip was forced to take action. Though the pair escaped prison time, Friar Folques was demoted and relocated to another department. As for Bishop Castanet, he was fined 20,000 livres and stripped of his title, putting his reign over Albi to an end.

While Carcassonne and the neighboring territories experienced a noticeable decrease in heresy-related arrests in the years that followed, Bernard's defiance of the Catholic Church would not go unpunished. In December 1319, Bernard was arrested on the charge of obstruction of the Inquisition and treason against the French crown. What became of him is still unknown. Some say he was marched to the gallows alongside his cortege. Others say he spent the rest of his life chained and miserable in the cold dungeons of Carcassonne.

The Catholic Church's unhealthy obsession with the heretics eventually petered out in the mid-14th century, but before people Carcassonne could even catch their breath, the site was bombarded with another, even more harrowing batch of problems. In the 1320s, the "Great Mortality," better known as the plague, struck Carcassonne, claiming the lives of anywhere between 30-50% of the population. The severe famine that ensued continued to pick at what remained of the Carcassonnians.

As bad as those problems were, it was Carcassonne's involuntary involvement in the Hundred Years' War that would truly threaten its existence. The campaigns of Edward "the Black Prince" of Woodstock led him to Carcassonne in early November 1355. Despite the clear signs of a deteriorating city being neglected by the vanishing population, Prince Edward was mesmerized by the sight of it: "It was a fair city to look upon, and a great one. It was larger, stronger, and more beautiful than York."

When the prince failed to take hold of the armed fortress, he set his eyes upon the Ville Basse. The residents of the lower town begged him to leave their already ailing town, and they even offered him 250,000 gold crowns (roughly $53,123 USD today) to sweeten the deal. But Edward was not interested in any of their inducements; after all, he was here to "deliver justice." An extract from a letter written by the Black Prince himself summed up what followed: "We spent the whole day in burning, so that [the Ville Basse] was completely destroyed."

A depiction of the Black Prince

To say that the destruction was catastrophic would be an understatement. As one of the prince's fellow commanders, Sir John Wingfield, later put it, "There was never such loss nor destruction as hath been in this raid."

Modern Developments

"Carcassonne, a memory full of glory,

Radiant name in a sky of clarity,

Let's learn to read your great story,

In front of the towers of the ancient city." – J.F. Jeanjean, "Carcassounéso"

In 1659, the Treaty of the Pyrenees, which was finalized at the Pheasant Island on by the Bidasoa River, settled what had become a centuries-long territorial dispute between the French and Spanish sovereigns. As stipulated by the historic treaty, Roussillon, Perpignan, Carcassonne, and the 33 villages of the Cerdagne were granted to King Louis XIV of France. To balance out the Spanish territorial losses, King Philip IV of Spain was awarded the County of Barcelona and the historic villa of Llívia. Additionally, the French king vowed to renounce his support for Portugal, and he further agreed to a strategic union with Princess Maria Theresa of Spain, the daughter of his nemesis. In exchange for a hefty dowry, Maria Theresa was expected to withdraw herself from the queue to the Spanish crown. This dowry, however, was never settled, a major factor that led to the War of Devolution 9 years later.

Following the implementation of the treaty, the official military command center of the French government was transferred from Carcassonne to Perpignan. All frontier fortresses, including the hilltop citadel and the Five Sons of Carcassonne, were deserted and left to collect dust. As time progressed, local builders began to pilfer stones and other materials of varying sizes from the Cité rubble, recycling them as construction materials for new buildings. With the military chapter of its history now closed, the Carcassonnians were allowed to direct their focus to the local industries.

In October 1666, the newly-appointed French Minister of Finances, Jean-Baptiste Colbert, commissioned the construction of the Canal du Mudi. This 223 mile complex of man-made waterways, interspersed with 328 aqueducts, bridges, locks, tunnels, and more, was designed by Pierre-Paul Riquet. The canal, which flowed through the heart of Carcassonne, connected the Mediterranean to the Atlantic, thereby serving as the perfect platform for the thriving trades to grow.

By the 1800s, the hilltop fortress in the Cité had become nothing more than a glorified military base, inhabited by only a handful of royal soldiers at a time to guard the small arsenal Napoleon had installed there. On the other side of the River Aude, the Ville Basse had evolved into a bustling residential and industrial center that specialized in wool, wine, liqueur, and wheat.

The decaying fortress atop the hill had fallen into such disuse that the French government began to make preparations for its disassembly in 1849, only to be swamped with protests from locals who wished to preserve their "national heritage." By 1853, respected historian Jean-Pierre Cros-Meyrevieille, the president of the newly formed Administration of the Arts, had garnered more than enough support and funds from wealthy patrons to restore the fortress. Local architect Viollet le Duc, who was assigned to oversee the project, defended the restorations, asserting, "I doubt that there exists anywhere in Europe as complete and formidable a system of defense of the 6th, 12th, and 13th centuries, as interesting a subject or study, and more picturesque situation."

One of Viollet's students, Paul Boeswillwald, inherited the responsibility of supervising the restorations upon the death of his mentor.

A late 19th century picture of Carcassonne

Another architect by the name of Nodet would later pick up where Boeswillwald had left off. In the early 1960s, several of the towers were rebuilt into U-shaped structures, overlaid with soft, pink brick, and crowned with "sloping, terracotta tiled roofs" so as to reflect a more traditional, Romanesque style.

In 1996, the Canal du Midi was formally classified as a UNESCO World Heritage site, and the same distinction was awarded to the Medieval Cité a year later. Today, nearly 50,000 residents (including the 50 or so who reside in the mdeival city) call Carcassonne home, making it the second-most populated city in the Aude, after Narbonne.

Online Resources

Other books about Carcassonne on Amazon

Bibliography

Editors, S. T. (2016, June 2). The Story of Lady Carcas. Retrieved January 25, 2018, from https://thestorytellershat.com/2016/06/02/the-story-of-lady-carcas/

Editors, C. L. (2015). Carcassonne – A tale of two Languedoc towns. Retrieved January 25, 2018, from http://www.creme-de-languedoc.com/Languedoc/city-guides/carcassonne.php

Editors, F. F. (2015, October 17). 10 Facts About Carcassonne. Retrieved January 25, 2018, from https://factfile.org/10-facts-about-carcassonne

Editors, A. O. (2011). La Cité Médiévale de Carcassonne. Retrieved January 25, 2018, from https://www.atlasobscura.com/places/la-cite-mediavale-de-carcassonne

Mach, A. (2014). 10 Amazing Facts About the French Medieval City of Carcassonne. Retrieved January 25, 2018, from http://fiveminutehistory.com/10-amazing-facts-french-medieval-city-carcassonne/

Editors, T. P. (2016, January 22). On This Spot: France's Flying Pig of Carcassonne. Retrieved January 25, 2018, from http://www.nola.com/travel/index.ssf/2016/01/on_this_spot_the_flying_pig_of.html

Editors, T. C. (2012). The Legend of Dame Carcas. Retrieved January 25, 2018, from http://www.tourism-carcassonne.co.uk/discover/history-carcassonne/legend-dame-carcas

Editors, T. C. (2014). History of Carcassonne. Retrieved January 25, 2018, from http://www.tourism-carcassonne.co.uk/discover/history-carcassonne

Munson, S. (2015). Visiting Carcassonne: France's famous Medieval Walled City. Retrieved January 25, 2018, from https://www.francetravelguide.com/visiting-carcassonne-frances-famous-medieval-walled-city.html

Editors, U. (2016). Historic Fortified City of Carcassonne. Retrieved January 25, 2018, from http://whc.unesco.org/en/list/345

Editors, W. W. (2012, June 18). Preview: Carcassonne. Retrieved January 25, 2018, from http://www.nevworldwonders.com/2012/06/preview-carcassonne.html

Palau, P., Benoist, P., Cadet, P., & Roche, J. (2017). CARCASSONNE WORLD HERITAGE SITE. Retrieved January 25, 2018, from http://de.media.france.fr/sites/default/files/document/press_kit/Carcassonne_Press%20pack_EN_2017.pdf

Editors, D. B. (2012, February 9). Petit Bonus : Dame Carcas......La légende ? Retrieved January 25, 2018, from http://www.divagations-et-balades.com/article-petit-bonus-la-dame-carcas-la-legende-98945273.html

Editors, M. (2007). La Legende de Dame Carcas. Retrieved January 25, 2018, from http://mescladis.free.fr/dame-carcas.htm

Editors, P. O. (2011). The Aude - Carcassonne . Retrieved January 25, 2018, from http://www.panoccitania.com/aude2.html

Editors, D. C. (2017). Discovering the famous Dame Carcas legend. Retrieved January 25, 2018, from http://www.tourisme-carcassonne.com/news/english-news/copy_of_outdoor-pleasures

Luzi, G. (2017, February 9). 6 Spectacular Things to See & Do in La Cité, Carcassonne. Retrieved January 25, 2018, from https://theculturetrip.com/europe/france/articles/6-spectacular-things-to-see-do-in-la-cite-carcassonne/

Riding, A. (1997, August 24). Carcassonne, City of Stone. Retrieved January 25, 2018, from http://www.nytimes.com/1997/08/24/travel/carcassonne-city-of-stone.html

Hurtado-Ròs, S., & Zuchetto, G. (2010). La légende de Dame Carcas à Carcassonne. Retrieved January 25, 2018, from http://www.patrimoinevivantdelafrance.fr/index.php?mact=News,cntnt01,detail,0&cntnt01articleid=39&cntnt01returnid=27

Editors, L. M. (2008, September 24). Carcassonne, The medieval walled city. Retrieved January 25, 2018, from http://lcmccabe.blogspot.tw/2008/09/carcassonne-medieval-walled-city.html

Sudakov, D. (2013, August 19). Pig as weapon of psychological attack. Retrieved January 25, 2018, from http://www.pravdareport.com/society/stories/19-08-2013/125425-pig_psychological_attack-0/

Editors, C. M. (2010). Gates & Barbicans. Retrieved January 25, 2018, from http://www.castlesandmanorhouses.com/architecture_04_gates.htm

Editors, C. L. (2015). A guide to the citadel of Carcassonne. Retrieved January 25, 2018, from http://www.creme-de-languedoc.com/Languedoc/sightseeing/carcassonne-citadel.php

Editors, E. B. (2017, October 16). Carcassonne. Retrieved January 25, 2018, from https://www.britannica.com/place/Carcassonne

Editors, C. T. (2017). History of the Château Comtal in the Medieval City of Carcassonne. Retrieved January 25, 2018, from https://castles.today/france/carcassone/history/

Carr, K. (2017, July 30). Carcassonne – medieval castles. Retrieved January 25, 2018, from https://quatr.us/medieval/carcassonne-medieval-castles.htm

Editors, L. (2016). Location and History of Carcassonne (continued). Retrieved January 25, 2018, from http://www.lechappeebelle.co.uk/history.html

Editors, L. F. (2015). Historic Cities: Carcassonne . Retrieved January 25, 2018, from http://www.languedoc-france.info/030101_carcassonne.htm

Editors, L. F. (2015). The History of the Languedoc: the Celts. Retrieved January 25, 2018, from http://www.languedoc-france.info/1002_celts.htm

Editors, M. F. (2015). The Pre-Roman Period. Retrieved January 25, 2018, from http://www.midi-france.info/03010101_carcassonne.htm

Editors, B. (2012). The Gallo-Roman era. Retrieved January 26, 2018, from http://bbcp.pagesperso-orange.fr/english/cite/archimed/architecture.html#1

Editors, G. C. (2017). Une occupation humaine très ancienne. Retrieved January 26, 2018, from http://www.grandsite-carcassonne.fr/en/lhistoire

Editors, B. (2012). History of the walled city of Carcassonne: The Origins. Retrieved January 26, 2018, from http://bbcp.pagesperso-orange.fr/english/cite/histoire/hist.html

Editors, E. B. (2017, October 27). Neolithic Period. Retrieved January 26, 2018, from https://www.britannica.com/event/Neolithic-Period

German, S., PhD. (2014). The Neolithic Revolution. Retrieved January 26, 2018, from https://www.khanacademy.org/humanities/ap-art-history/global-prehistory-ap/paleolithic-mesolithic-neolithic/a/the-neolithic-revolution

Editors, W. A. (2016). Carcassonne Castle. Retrieved January 26, 2018, from https://en.wikiarquitectura.com/building/carcassonne-castle/

Editors, T. F. (2016, April 8). Visigothic. Retrieved January 26, 2018, from https://francetaste.wordpress.com/2016/04/08/visigothic/

Field, H. (2013, June 23). Carcassonne in South West France – Sleeping Beauty's 'real life' castle? Retrieved January 26, 2018, from https://www.vintagetravel.co.uk/blog/carcassonne-in-south-west-france-sleeping-beautys-real-life-castle/

Editors, T. C. (2017, June 20). When – and why – did people first start using money? Retrieved January 26, 2018, from https://theconversation.com/when-and-why-did-people-first-start-using-money-78887

Editors, M. (2015). History of Carcassonne. Retrieved January 26, 2018, from http://mescladis.free.fr/ANGLAIS/pages%20html/history.htm

Editors, C. (2011). THE ROMAN TOWN OF CARCASO. Retrieved January 26, 2018, from http://www.carcassonne.culture.fr/en/hc200.htm

Bailey, R. (2015). Guide to Carcassonne and Surrounding Region. Retrieved January 26, 2018, from http://www.rosemarybailey.com/travel-writing-2/carcassonne-and-surrounding-region/

Labate, V. (2016, August 31). Roman walls. Retrieved January 26, 2018, from https://www.ancient.eu/article/942/roman-walls/

Editors, P. P. (2004). What Happened in A.D. 508? Retrieved January 26, 2018, from http://www.patmospapers.com/daniel/in508.htm

Hardy, F. W. (2016, October 10). Clovis and the Year AD 508 . Retrieved January 26, 2018, from http://www.historicism.org/Documents/Clovis_and_508.pdf

Editors, W. T. (2002). The Baptism of Clovis—1,500 Years of Catholicism in France. Retrieved January 26, 2018, from https://wol.jw.org/en/wol/d/r1/lp-e/2002165

Wasson, D. L. (2014, November 10). Clovis I. Retrieved January 26, 2018, from https://www.ancient.eu/Clovis_I/

Editors, H. W. (2001). The Franks. Retrieved January 26, 2018, from http://history-world.org/franks.htm

Jaffus, F. (2017). CARCASSONNE AND THE TREASURE OF ROME. Retrieved January 29, 2018, from https://www.rhedesium.com/la-citeacute-de-carcassonne.html

Editors, M. F. (2012). The History of the Languedoc: The Moors (or Saracens). Retrieved January 29, 2018, from http://www.midi-france.info/1011_moors.htm

Norwich, J. J. (2007). Carcassonne . Retrieved January 29, 2018, from http://www.colindaylinks.com/france/carcassonne.html

Editors, E. T. (2012). Carcassonne – Medieval City. Retrieved January 29, 2018, from http://www.europeanadventuretravel.com/carcassonne-medieval-city/

Hosey, B. (2015, Spring). Carcassonne: A Medieval Citadel Rich in Historical Eloquence. Retrieved January 29, 2018, from https://scholarlycommons.obu.edu/cgi/viewcontent.cgi?referer=https://www.google.com.tw/&httpsredir=1&article=1019&context=history

Editors, N. L. (2009). VISCOUNT OF CARCASSONNE. Retrieved January 29, 2018, from http://netlibrary.net/articles/Viscount_of_Carcassonne

Editors, T. C. (2016). The Medieval City. Retrieved January 29, 2018, from http://www.tourism-carcassonne.co.uk/discover/parks-and-outdoor-spaces/medieval-city

Editors, D. W. (2017). Basilica of St. Nazaire and St. Celse, Carcassonne. Retrieved January 29, 2018, from https://www.discoverworld.com/France/Occitania/Aude/Arrondissement-of-Carcassonne/Carcassonne/Basilica-of-St-Nazaire-and-St-Celse:In-depth#Architecture

Editors, G. Q. (2010). What is Arianism? Retrieved January 29, 2018, from https://www.gotquestions.org/arianism.html

Editors, G. D. (2006, March). Newton's Arian beliefs. Retrieved January 29, 2018, from http://www-groups.dcs.st-and.ac.uk/history/Extras/Newton_Arian.html

Editors, R. (2018, January 27). Salian Frankish Mythology. Retrieved January 29, 2018, from https://www.revolvy.com/main/index.php?s=Salian%20Frankish%20Mythology&item_type=topic

Cavendish, R. (2011, November 11). Death of Clovis I of the Franks. Retrieved January 29, 2018, from http://www.historytoday.com/richard-cavendish/death-clovis-i-franks

Editors, R. (2017, March 31). County of Carcassonne . Retrieved January 29, 2018, from https://www.revolvy.com/main/index.php?s=County%20of%20Carcassonne

Editors, E. (2005). Ermengard of Carcassonne. Retrieved January 29, 2018, from https://epistolae.ctl.columbia.edu/woman/25489.html

Cheyette, F. L. (1988, October). The "Sale" of Carcassonne to the Counts of Barcelona (1067-1070) and the Rise of the Trencavels. Retrieved January 29, 2018, from http://www.journals.uchicago.edu/doi/abs/10.2307/2853537?journalCode=spc

Editors, L. F. (2011). The House of Trencavel. Retrieved January 29, 2018, from http://www.languedoc-france.info/1914_trencavel.htm

Editors, T. S. (2009, September 9). Viscount's Castle, La Bastide St. Louis and Cathars in Carcassonne. Retrieved January 29, 2018, from https://travelswithsheila.com/the_carcassonne_france_viscoun.html

Editors, M. (2013). Les chantes traditionnels. Retrieved January 29, 2018, from http://mescladis.free.fr/chants.htm

Editors, C. (2016). Cathars and Cathar Beliefs in the Languedoc Béatrice de Planissolles, Testimony to the Inquisition. Retrieved January 29, 2018, from http://www.cathar.info/121213_fournier_beatrice.htm

Editors, H. T. (2011, November 27). Cathar Heresy – Count Raymond VI of Toulouse. Retrieved January 29, 2018, from http://historytimeshistory.blogspot.tw/2011/11/cathar-heresy-count-raymond-vi-of.html

Editors, C. (2016). Who's Who In The Cathar War. Retrieved January 29, 2018, from http://www.cathar.info/cathar_whoswho.htm

Cavendish, R. (2009, August 8). Carcassonne falls in the Albigensian Crusade. Retrieved January 29, 2018, from http://www.historytoday.com/richard-cavendish/carcassonne-falls-albigensian-crusade

Editors, C. C. (2016). History - Carcassonne. Retrieved January 30, 2018, from http://www.catharcastles.info/carcassonne.php#history

Editors, M. (2013). The House of the Inquisition. Retrieved January 30, 2018, from http://mescladis.free.fr/ANGLAIS/pages%20html/house-inquisition.htm

Pegg, M. G. (2005, April 2). The Hammer of the Inquisitors: Brother Bernard Delicieux and the Struggle Against the Inquisition in Fourteenth-Century France. Retrieved January 30, 2018, from https://muse.jhu.edu/article/183786

Editors, R. (2018, January 10). Cathar castles . Retrieved January 30, 2018, from https://www.revolvy.com/main/index.php?s=Cathar%20castles&item_type=topic

Editors, S. (2015, October 11). Crusaders Defeat Raymond II of Trencavel in His Attempt to Recapture Carcassone . Retrieved January 30, 2018, from http://skepticism.info/timeline/october-history/9081-crusaders-defeat-raymond-ii-trencavel-attempt-recapture-carcassone.html

Cros-Mayrevieille, J. P. (2016). Carcassonne, Le Pont Vieux. Retrieved January 30, 2018, from http://www.odeaanaude.eu/cataloguade2/carcassonne-le-pont-vieux-p-359.html?language=en

Axelrod, L. (2012). The Walled City of Carcassonne in Languedoc, France. Retrieved January 30, 2018, from https://european-history.knoji.com/the-walled-city-of-carcassonne-in-languedoc-france/

Editors, H. E. (2013, January). The Black Prince: hero or villain? Retrieved January 30, 2018, from http://www.historyextra.com/period/medieval/the-black-prince-hero-or-villain/

Editors, M. N. (2009, January 4). Guide to Carcassonne. Retrieved January 30, 2018, from http://www.medievalists.net/2009/01/guide-to-carcassone/

Editors, S. S. (2012, June 12). The Fortified City of Carcassonne. Retrieved January 30, 2018, from http://southweststory.com/tourist-attractions/the-fortified-city-of-carcassonne

Editors, I. P. (2014, September 2). Carcassonne, medieval anti-Semitism and the Black Death. Retrieved January 30, 2018, from http://irishhistorypodcast.ie/carcassonne-medieval-anti-semitism-and-the-black-death/

Editors, M. F. (2013). The History of the Languedoc: The Treaty of the Pyrenees. Retrieved January 30, 2018, from http://www.midi-france.info/1010_treaty.htm

Editors, U. (2015). Canal du Midi. Retrieved January 30, 2018, from http://whc.unesco.org/en/list/770

Charyn, J. (2017). *Little Angel Street*. Head of Zeus, Ltd.

McDonald, N. (2013). *Mysteries of The Cathar Country*. Lulu.Com.

Geography of France. (1992). PediaPress.

Thompson, J. W. (2016). *History of the Middle Ages: 300-1500*. Routledge.

Cowper, M. (2012). *Cathar Castles: Fortresses of the Albigensian Crusade 1209–1300*. Bloomsbury Publishing.

Jones, M. (2017). *The Black Prince: The King That Never Was*. Head of Zeus, Ltd.

O'Shea, S. (2011). *The Friar of Carcassonne: The Last Days of the Cathars*. Profile Books.

Worker, J. (2016). *Travels through History - France*. Andrews UK, Ltd.

Graham-Leigh, E. (2005). *The Southern French Nobility and the Albigensian Crusade*. The Boydell Press.

O'Shea, Stephen (2011). *The Friar Of Carcassonne*. Vancouver, BC, Canada: Douglas & McIntyre.

Maland M.A., David (1991). Europe in the Seventeenth Century *(Second ed.)*. Macmillan. p.277

Free Books by Charles River Editors

We have brand new titles available for free most days of the week. To see which of our titles are currently free, click on this link.

Discounted Books by Charles River Editors

We have titles at a discount price of just 99 cents everyday. To see which of our titles are currently 99 cents, click on this link.

Printed in Great Britain
by Amazon